ARE YOU THINKING YOURSELF INTO LOWER INTELLIGENCE?

By David Curran

CHAPTERS

AN INTRODUCTION	5
COMMUNICATION AND INTELLIGENCE	11
INTELLIGENCE, WHAT IS IT?	23
THE MYSTIQUE OF INTELLIGENCE	24
ORDERING OUR APPROACH TO PROBLEMS	27
SYMPTOMS	31
SOME BASIC RULES OF PROBLEM SOLVING	35
PRACTICE PROBLEMS	39
RELIGIOUS BELIEF AND LOGIC	44
WOMEN AND INTELLIGENCE	46
IQ	48
NOTES ON TEST TAKING	51
HIGH TEST ANXIETY	55
ANSWERS TO PRACTICE PROBLEMS	58
CONCLUSION	62
END NOTES	62

THIS BOOK IS DEDICATED TO MY WIFE PATRICIA WHO IS THE SMARTEST WOMAN I HAVE EVER KNOWN.

© COPYRIGHT MCMLXXVI, MMMCMXCIX DAVID F CURRAN

CHAPTER ONE: AN INTRODUCTION

Are you thinking yourself into lower intelligence? The following is a true story about an individual whose goals may seem to differ from yours. Keep in mind that he could just as easily be about a laborer who doesn't think he can become a television repair technician, or a housewife who doesn't think she can do auto repair. You, like the individual in this story, may have more intelligence than you give yourself credit for. You, like him, may have more potential than your previous accomplishments would indicate.

Figure 1. How we are nurtured or how we nurture ourselves has an influence on how intelligent we think we are.

Long before entering high school this student had been interested in pursuing a career in chemistry. He did not do well in the more complex forms of high school math and believed he never would. Because of this he entered business school in college. He, in freshman year, reluctantly took the required math course. In this simplest of college math courses he was initially doing only average work. By chance his curriculum led him to take a course in cultural anthropology. In studying primitive cultures he discovered two things, which changed his life.

Figure 2. Many so-called primitive languages are far more complex than English. Yet most children learn to speak their native language.

The first was that:

- ALMOST ALL THE PEOPLE IN THESE CULTURES WERE ABLE TO UNDERSTAND THE LANGUAGE, EVEN THOUGH SOME OF THE LANGUAGES WERE MORE COMPLEX THAN ENGLISH.

Figure 3. Language is the weakest link in the chain of understanding even the most complex ideas.

The second was that:

- LANGUAGE IS THE LIMITING FACTOR--IT IS THE WEAKEST LINK IN THE CHAIN OF UNDERSTANDING EVEN THE MOST COMPLEX IDEAS.

From this he drew two conclusions:

- AN IDEA CANNOT BE SO COMPLICATED THAT IT CANNOT BE COMMUNICATED BY LANGUAGE.

- AN IDEA CANNOT BE MORE DIFFICULT TO LEARN THAN THE LANGUAGE IT IS IN.[i]

Figure 4. Curiosity can help bridge communication boundaries.

With a sudden confidence generated by this idea the student started asking even silly questions in math class and vastly improved his grade. He then transferred into the school of science as a chemistry major. There was a required math course he needed to transfer into the chemistry program, calculus. With the help of a great teacher[ii], and his new philosophy, he did 'A' work.

This student's problem had been that he, like many people, did not have a realistic view of his own intelligence. For us to avoid this mistake we need to examine our own concepts about intelligence, to determine if we are, in fact, thinking ourselves into lower intelligence.

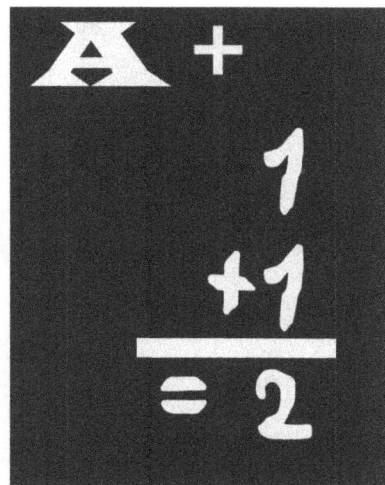

Figure 5. Did you know in math addition, subtraction, multiplication and division is all there is. Every higher form of math just uses these in interesting ways.

QUESTIONS FOR THOUGHT

Are there subjects or ideas you don't believe you have the ability to master or understand? Make a list of these. Ask yourself if it is because you cannot understand them, or because they have not been presented in a way you can understand?

Can you think of an idea too complicated to be communicated? Would it have any real value?

Figure 6. Cherish the time you spend thinking.

CHAPTER TWO: COMMUNICATION AND INTELLIGENCE

Our lack of ability in, and ignorance of communication plays a great part in our distortions of the idea of intelligence. We believe that because we understand the language we are masters at communicating with it, and are as masterful as we ever need to become. When someone communicates an idea to us (assuming we are paying attention and interested in it) we either immediately understand it or assume one of three things:

Figure 7. Communication like painting, requires thought, patience and practice.

- It is a subject we don't know enough about to make sense of.

- The speaker does not know what he or she is talking about, and not making any sense.

- We are not intelligent or smart enough to understand it.

- Figure 8. Thinking you are not smart enough to understand something, is like thinking you have a pea sized brain! If you did you never would have learned the language you speak.

The second assumption could imply the first. And the first sometimes implies the third. But the third assumption is the dangerous one. But if we think we are not smart enough to understand an idea, we are in the worst possible situation. Why might we think this way?

We might think this way because we are ignorant of our own intelligence. We might think this because of our ignorance of, and history of problems in communication.

Figure 9. What if no one understood Einstein?

I've heard lines in television shows and movies that would imply Einstein was the only one who understood his own theory. Yet, we know this is not possible. In order for a scientist to have his work accepted, let alone have that work make him famous, the scientist must convince others of its validity. Ideas only one person can understand are the ideas of madmen (or screenwriters). Yet most of us believe, at least in part, that there are ideas we ourselves and others cannot understand. We have allowed ourselves to acquire an awe of certain ideas.

The groundwork for this awe of ideas may have be laid at an early age by well meaning parents. The words "You wouldn't understand it," and "you can't do that," build the belief that there are things beyond one's capability and intelligence. Few parents have the skill and/or patience to answer every childhood question in an unharmful way. In fact, our parents' parents were probably guilty of the same thing. Perhaps the subject that needs explaining is too personal. Perhaps it would scare the child. Perhaps the answer would take too much time. Yet, as children, we do not even guess at these unvoiced reasons. We take the remarks as given, perhaps even given with love, as definitions of our own ability. Then carry these hindering definitions, throughout our lives.

Figure 10. Love can inadvertently squash intelligence.

As adults we continue on our own. When we find subjects difficult, time-consuming, boring, or we are too plain lazy to tackle them, we tell ourselves we can't understand this or that. And this is just a convenient excuse for giving up. We use the excuse so often we begin to believe we cannot understand certain things. We are miscommunicating with ourselves. We are thinking ourselves into lower intelligence because of an awe created out of ignorance.

Although technology is advancing skillful communication is an art that is rather unpracticed by the masses. There are a great many erroneous ideas that inhibit our self-evaluation of our intelligence directly or indirectly.

For Example:

Figure 11. Though a good teacher understands, not everyone who understands can teach. The best teachers understand how they learned. (My apologies to old E here.)

Many of us believe that a knowledge of a subject also implies an ability to impart that knowledge to others.

This is entirely incorrect. An expert who does not realize that he is not capable of explaining a subject to someone not on his level of experience can be damaging to himself and the person he tries explaining it to. The expert may not realize he is having communication problems. The nuclear physicist does not need to explain fission to the grocer in order to survive. He or she doesn't even need to explain it to his or her spouse to insure a happy marriage.

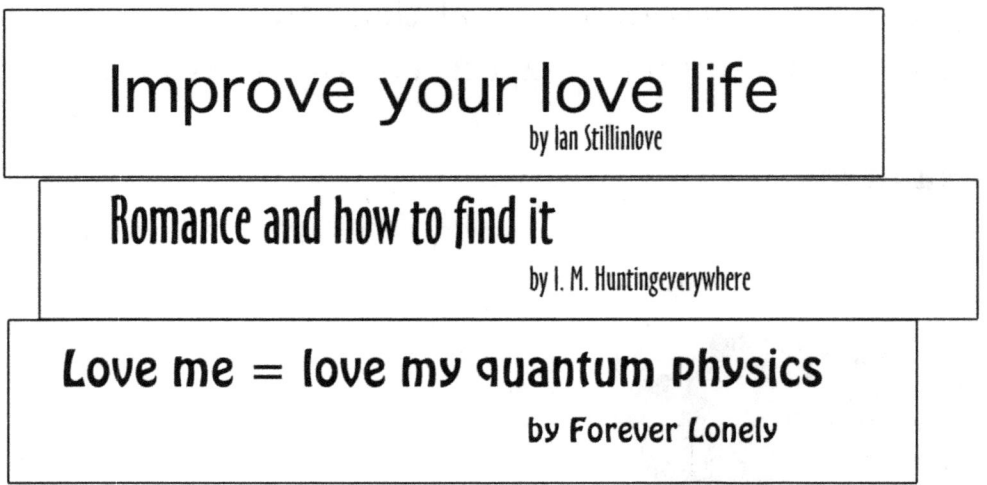

Figure 12. Fortunately, we don't have to understand everything to live and enjoy life. Unfortunately, not everyone knows how to teach what they do understand.

If we ourselves are not physicists or philosophers, and try to communicate with one about their respective fields, it is very likely both parties will be frustrated. The worst feelings, however, will be on our part. Especially if we do not realize the expert may not have the time for a lengthy discussion, nor the skill to explain what has taken him years to learn in a way we can understand.

Figure 13. Taking on things we are not ready for is like trying to encourage a baby to ride a motorcycle.

We would not be bothered if we didn't understand a story read to us in Chinese unless we studied that language. Yet, many experts can make some of us feel inferior simply because they speak the same language we do.[iii] We should not expect to understand things that require time and study, easily. Yet, many of us do, and end up thinking ourselves into lower intelligence.

Most of us may not try to understand physicists, or philosophers. We deal with people on a level closer to our own. Still, there can be a world of difference between a pharmacist and an auto mechanic. We should be aware that problems will develop even among people in the same field, simply because we are human, and have both faults and egos.

Figure 14. To master any subject, from math to auto repair, you can't be afraid to ask questions.

For example, if a woman, taking a course in auto repair, sits through an evening's lesson and understands none of it, because she was afraid to ask a question on a minor point, she's at fault.[iv] Those who seem the most intelligent, the ones who are ahead of the game, are those who are not afraid of asking the stupidest questions.[v] The student from our first example, who eventually aced calculus with the help of a good teacher, remembers one turning point in his dummy math course, after coming to his epiphany via cultural anthropology. He asked his dummy math teacher the equivalent of why is 2 and 2 equal to 4. The teacher patiently explained that it was just a convention. Not only did the student understand what the teacher was explaining, he understood that his not being afraid to ask the question itself was a turning point.

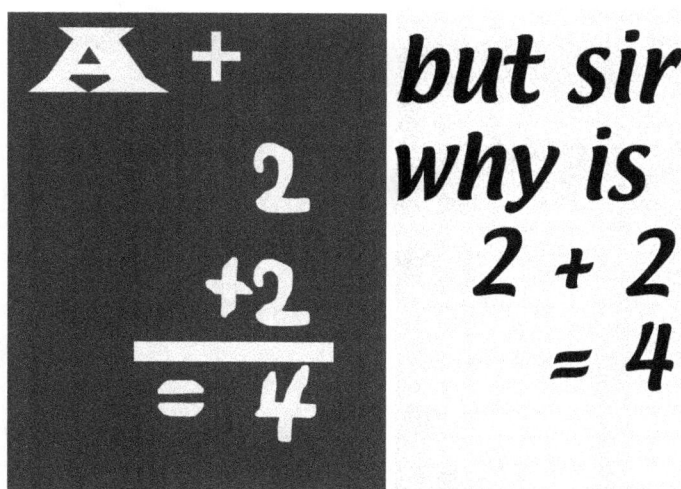

Figure 15. If you aren't afraid to ask seemingly stupid questions, no question will intimidate you.

Without communication we'd have no concept of intelligence. Communication is, however, a human invention and thus overloaded with faults.[vi] Primarily those faults center around the fact that in our basically competitive society most people like to give the impression that they are smarter than their fellow man.

Even otherwise honorable people will deliberately mislead you to protect the fact that they do not know something. Especially, when it is something they should know, or they think they should know. You may be guilty of this yourself. Have you ever used the phrase "you wouldn't understand."

Learn to recognize when people are doing this, i.e. pretending to know something they do not. And never let such situations make you feel inferior or insecure.

In competition part of the game is to "psych out' our opponent. Learning to do this can be an important part of winning. It is especially true in mental games such as chess, but can apply to all games and sports from poker to boxing.

You wouldn't understand.

Figure 16. Most people who use this as a mantra either have a vested interest in making you think they are smarter than you, or are simply not patient enough to explain it in a way you could understand.

Some people want to charge you higher prices for their services, or, as in this next example, want to continue getting your business.

An intelligent young man read up on how to tune his own car. He tuned it and in doing so made a very simple mistake. An electrical wire on his distributor was attached incorrectly. His car would not run, and when he checked over what he had done he was at a loss to discover what his mistake was.

After puzzling over it for some time he took the car to a service station. When he came back to pick up the car he asked, "What did I do wrong?" The station owner replied, you wouldn't understand. It was years before the fellow felt like trying to tune his car again, and only after someone had pointed out what his probable mistake had been.[vii]

Finally, there are people who flaunt their intelligence for the sake of itself. They just feel better if they can put everyone else down. They play carefully devised games that inflate their own egos. These people are intellectual birds of prey and should be avoided. [viii]

Human faults add to the mystique of intelligence. But before we can talk about this mystique, we need to define intelligence. We'll discuss that in the next chapter.

QUESTIONS FOR THOUGHT

- Make a list of all the ideas you can think of that would inhibit your self-evaluation of your intelligence.
- Have you ever been the victim of an expert who did not have the ability to communicate with you?[ix] Do you have any ideas about ways in which to spot these people?
- Why should you not be afraid to ask seemingly stupid questions? Do you believe that everyone, occasionally, finds even simple ideas presented in ways that are confusing to them?
- Make a list of situations in which people deliberately obscure communication for their own ends or try to make themselves look smarter than their fellow man. Use any real-life situations you've run across. Make up some imaginary situations if you haven't come across any.
- Look up the word affricate in a dictionary. Would you be able to use this word, being absolutely certain you were using it correctly without some additional help (i.e. looking up other words), or background knowledge. One problem with some dictionaries is

the fact that it is sometimes difficult to tell exactly how a word is used, and thus have a firm grasp of its meaning.

Chapter Three: INTELLIGENCE, WHAT IS IT?

Perhaps its is best to use an example. Suppose you have a four hundred piece puzzle that when completed, would form a picture of a beautiful woodland scene. We open the box, mix the pieces and then simply throw the pieces into the air. Is it likely the pieces will land as a completed puzzle or as a disordered mess? With our senses we perceive the world that throws its jigsaw puzzle of sensations at our senses. The ability to put in order the mess our senses perceive as the world is intelligence. Intelligence, very simply, is the ability to put ideas, perceptions, things in order.

 Food for Thought:

The second law of thermodynamics, in simple terms, states that all the energy in the universe tends toward disorder. In other words if you throw your puzzle into the air it will land as a disordered mess.[x] Our intelligence, our very existence is in contrast to this law. We use a great deal of energy, mostly chemical, to maintain the order, which is ourselves. If intelligence is the ability to put things in order, the only real measure of intelligence would be a measure of the energy available for this task!

Chapter Four: THE MYSTIQUE OF INTELLIGENCE

The mystique our world attributes to intelligence has given us erroneous idea about what intelligence is, does and will do. We've been taught that certain people are more intelligent than others. We've been led to believe that we can judge intelligence by certain achievements, accomplishments, and tests. Some people, for example, would consider a physicist more intelligent than a mountain man. Yet, is the ability to survive in the wilderness any less important than recognizing and remembering the way electrons are arranged around an atom? Should we look for a definition of intelligence along the lines of "some people are more intelligent."[xi]

Figure 17. If survival was our measure of intelligent, who is more intelligent in a snowy wilderness, a physicist or a mountain man?

What if we defined intelligence as the ability to survive? What would happen to our physicist if he were lost in the mountains? It may not be wise to try and judge whether the mountain man or physicist has better ordered their world. We cannot measure someone's ability to put their world in order by evaluating their world in relation to our own.

For most of us the world is one in which people[xii] like answers quickly and efficiently. Our intelligence is socially and personally measured by how quickly and efficiently we put things in order, using time limits and tests. If we don't demonstrate our ability in this way we are thought to have a lack of it.

Figure 18. Do tests with time limits really measure our potential, or what we have already learned?

Yet, does the fact that someone never learned to swim truthfully inform us that they cannot learn to swim? Our mistake is that no one ever asks us, and we never ask ourselves, "Would we have gotten the answer right if we had tried, if we had the necessary background, or if we have been given more time?" Instead, we believe that if we don't come up with an answer, or if we don't come up with one within a time limit, we have failed, and our intelligence is not up to par.[xiii] Here, lack of intelligence is not so much the problem as ignorance, ignorance that we have to develop the ability to use our intelligence as we develop the muscles of our body. We put ourselves down because we don't know enough about intelligence.

   Questions for Thought

Of the people you know: who is the most intelligent? Who is the least intelligent? Why? Is it fair to judge them this way? How well do you really know them?

Can we judge someone's intelligence by their role in society? Why or why not?

Have you ever, after failing at something, asked yourself, "Would I succeed if I keep trying, or if I give myself more time?"

Have you ever decided that your ability or your intelligence is not up to par?

Chapter Five: ORDERING OUR APPROACH TO PROBLEMS

Suppose, for example, we want to put together that jigsaw puzzle of a woodland scene mentioned earlier. We could take one piece, and then try to fit a piece to it by taking all the other pieces, one at time, until we find one that fits. We could then go through the pile again until we find one that fits these two, and so on, until we finish the puzzle. But will we have, if we are timed, or if given a time limit, completed it efficiently? Finding the borders first, or collecting pieces of the same color are some of the faster, more efficient methods of completing a jigsaw puzzle. But are we supposed to know automatically that some methods of completing the puzzle are more efficient than others?

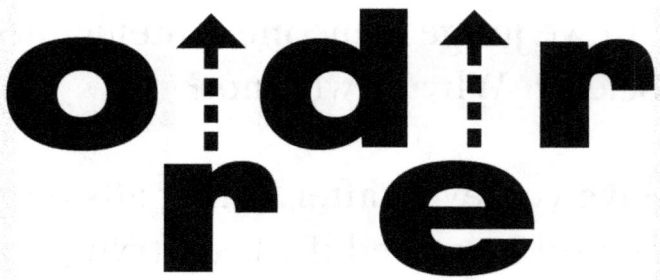

Figure 19. Ordering our approach to problems can help us solve them.

When we look for more efficient way of completing the puzzle we are doing more than just putting the puzzle together. WE HAVE BEGUN TO ORDER A MEANS OF PUTTING THE PUZZLE IN ORDER. The idea that we should order the way in which we approach problems is a concept which must be learned. Ordering the way we approach problems is the key to the most effective use of intelligence.

The people who seem the most intelligent are those who have worked hard at ordering their approach to problems. Being efficient in using intelligence is not unlike using your hands on a production line. Imagine you are on a production line where you assemble a small part of a machine. A person does not become efficient in production work until he has practiced it so much that it becomes an effective unconscious routine.

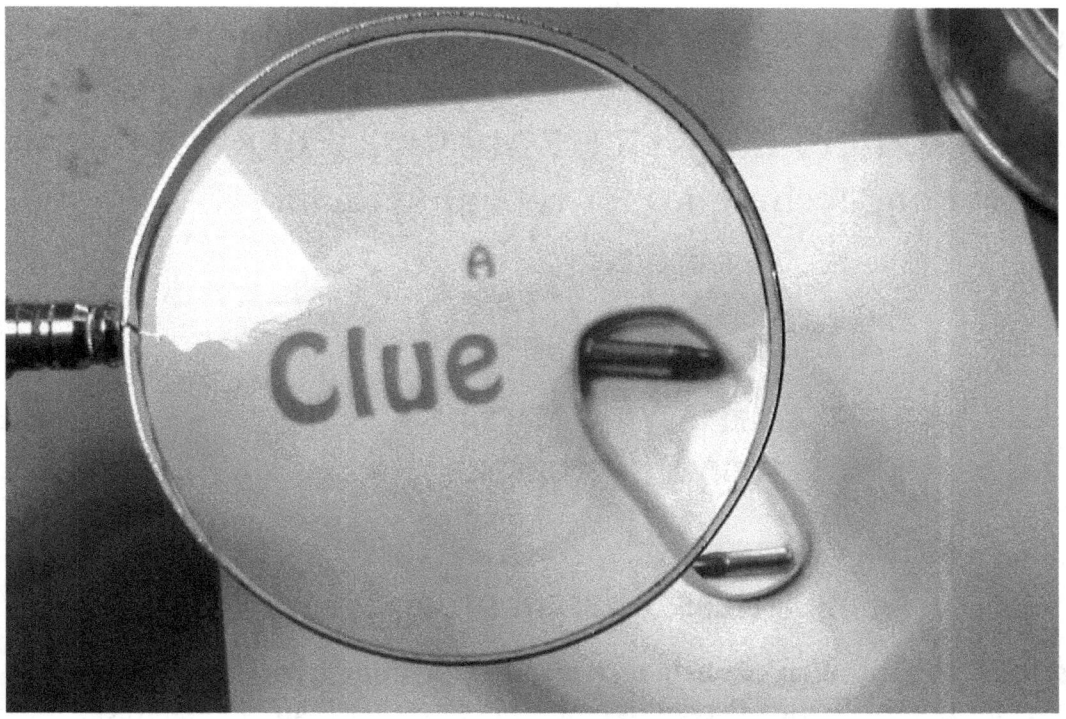

Figure 20. Whether working on an assembly line or doing detective work, it takes time to become proficient.

Sherlock Holmes, the famous fictional detective, amazed his friend Dr. Watson with his deductions. Yet, they seemed simple when explained. Sir Arthur Conan Doyle, Holmes' creator, explained in what is referred to as the 'canon'[xiv] by fans, that Holmes acquired the ability thru many years of practice.[xv]

But perhaps a real-life example would be better than a fictional one. Memory, ordered information, is an important aspect of intelligence. We have to be able to memorize things in order to communicate and solve problems. A lack of ability to memorize gives the impression of a lack of intelligence. But memory can be helped by an ordered approach to it. Books like Harry Lorayne & Jerry Lucas's THE MEMORY BOOK prove it by providing techniques for retaining memory.

Same letters different orders!

Figure 21. Organization can help us remember anything from random letters to important things. 'Smart Person' is easier to remember than 'tarsmonrsep.'

For example, when introduced to new people at a party, making up simple rhyming phrases based on the new person's name, while picturing that person involved in some aspect of the rhyme can vastly improve memory .

An erroneous idea that many of us have is that genius or super-intelligence is simply pushing a button and getting a correct answer. It sometimes seems that way, when we see something solve problems that have perplexed us, quickly. The truth is that that person has most likely practiced solving that type of problem or a related one.

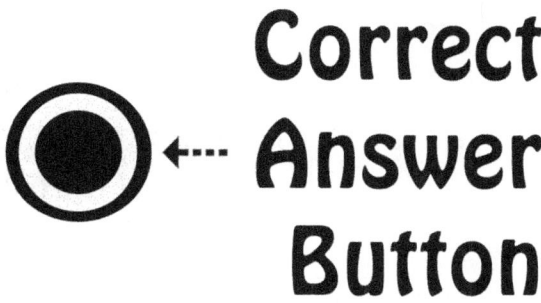

Figure 22. There is no magic button that gives anyone an instant answer. No one gets there without going the route.

A person practiced and proficient enough to know almost instinctively how to order problem-solving and put it to work, will indeed seem to perform magic. Yet, no such magic ever occurs. No one gets to the end of any journey, mental or physical without going the route.

Questions for thought:

Of those things that you have experienced that took time and practice to become proficient at, would you expect someone to pick them up instantly? We all meet people who seem super smart. What kind of ordering system, and/or practice do you think they might have had?

Whenever you encounter a task or problem of any kind, ask yourself, "Is this the best way to approach this?" Try to think of other methods.[xvi] Would any of these be better and if so why?

Create and note down a plan for judging the efficiency of any method of doing a given task. Try it whenever it applies. Revise and improve it as much as possible.

Chapter Six: SYMPTOMS OF THINKING YOURSELF INTO LOWER INTELLIGENCE

To show that practice is necessary to effectively order our approach to problems, perhaps we should look at a common situation. A friend presents us with a brain teaser problem. We assume we are as intelligent as our friend and should solve it rather quickly. Yet, if we believe that because we are intelligent we will quickly find an answer to the puzzle, without having to look into it too deeply, or order our approach to it, we are thinking ourselves into lower intelligence. Puzzles would not be 'puzzling' if they were easy to solve. All too often we don't consider the extent of the route we will have to follow in order to correctly solve the problem.

Figure 23. Solving a puzzle can seem as impossible as cracking a safe.

Let's look at what happens.

We try the first likely solution that comes to mind. It doesn't work. We try other likely solutions, but these don't work either. We fail to put any order at all to solving and end up going in circles. We repeat ways we have already tried because we lack the confidence that we have tried them correctly. Panic sets in. We begin to wonder if the puzzle is a hoax,[xvii] if it can really be solved. We may work ourselves so hard we become mentally fatigued. We get nowhere so we give up. We end up feeling inferior when we learn how simple the solution was. We make lame excuses. Or, maybe instead, we solve it after so long a time, that our lack of planning makes us feel it was only luck we found the correct solution.

MOST OF US HAVE EXPERIENCED THIS. Just think back to the last time you misplaced your car keys or other important object.[xviii]

Realizing that an orderly approach to problems is necessary can save us from frustrations like this. Practice and some thought lead people with demonstrated intelligence to practice some basic rules. The next chapter deals with those rules.

 Questions for Thought:

Make a list of the symptoms outlined in this chapter. Have you ever experienced them?

What is the first step one should take in approaching a problem?

How can you go about ordering your approach? Must you consider various different ways of tackling it?

If some ways of attacking a problem are better than others, will you only be able to learn which ways by experience? Do you think proven methods should be written about and published.

How often should we reevaluate our methods of attacking a problem?

Figure 24. Don't believe the old saying: 'If you can keep your head while everyone around you is losing their's, you don't understand the seriousness of the problem.'

What signs of panic should we look for? When these occur should we continue, or come back to the problem at a later time?

If putting a problem away and coming back to it later is not a cop-out, and is, in fact, a wise decision in view of the fact that we can become mentally fatigued, how can you tell when you are mentally fatigued?

Chapter Seven: SOME BASIC RULES OF PROBLEM SOLVING

- The most important rule is to have confidence in your ability to solve a problem. Without confidence your attempt to solve any problem is doomed to failure.

- Never apply to yourself any unnecessary time limits. There are instances in which they will be applied to you, but never apply any to yourself. You should remember that each attempt at problem solving you make, will increase your ability to problem solve in the future.

- Order your approach to problem solving so that you check each answer once and only once, and if it does not work you may confidently discard it. Don't run around in circles afraid you've missed something (or hoping against hope you have). This may seem obvious but how often have you done this when looking for a lost object.

- Do not attempt problem solving unless you want to solve the problem and are willing to spend the time to collect the information needed to solve it, and to solve it. Intelligent people do not attempt problems that would merely be a waste of their time. Learn to spot those 'wastes of time' beforehand. It's a bad idea to start on a problem and then use 'it's a waste of time' as an excuse for giving up. The dangers of this were mentioned in chapter two.

Figure 25. Don't let imaginary rules crowd out or bully your ideas.

o Never limit your ideas by any other rules than those stated in the problem. When the rules that govern your everyday life do not work in a problem, discard them, and build an order of new rules. Very often, in puzzles especially, the rules are meant to trick you. The rules are stated in such a way as to make you think you cannot do something you may do. Or, deliberately steer you away from the right solution. This may seem a cheap trick, but it is in a way a benefit. The rules of nature and life can be just as tricky. Just imagine for example you are walking down a road looking for a shortcut to a town that is a hundred yards to your immediate left. The road runs parallel to the town and finally makes a U-turn one mile ahead that will take you to the town. If you can't find a short cut you will have to travel two miles. As you walk along you pass a lot with a line of painted rocks labeled 'no trespassing.' Next you pass a lot with a high hedge, then a lot with a tall wooden fence. After that you pass a lot with a metal fence that has barbed wire at the top. You are so used to fences and boundaries of one kind or another that when you pass a row of trees growing along the road you assume this is a fence also, when, in fact, the trees just grew there naturally and the lot owner would have no problem with people taking a short cut through his yard. In this example it is our own nature and inclination to look for signs that has tricked us. To not fall prey to this kind of thinking, it helps to have had some practice, and personal insight into what is often called 'thinking outside of the box.'

- Practice! The more you try the better you will become. Some sample puzzles are given in the next chapter. And you can always find books on puzzles at the library.

 Questions for Thought:

If you lack confidence that you have the ability to solve any puzzle try to soul search and find out why. Is it because of repeated failures? We all fail. You can expect to fail. But you should never let any failure discourage you. Try to treat each failure as an individual thing. It is not the failure that discourages us but a lack of confidence engendered by that failure. Remember that problems often look difficult, but what did it take when you were a young child to learn the language you are reading now?

Chapter Eight: PRACTICE PROBLEMS

The problems presented here have been around for some time. I have merely added my personal touch to their presentation.[xix]

One: Snakes

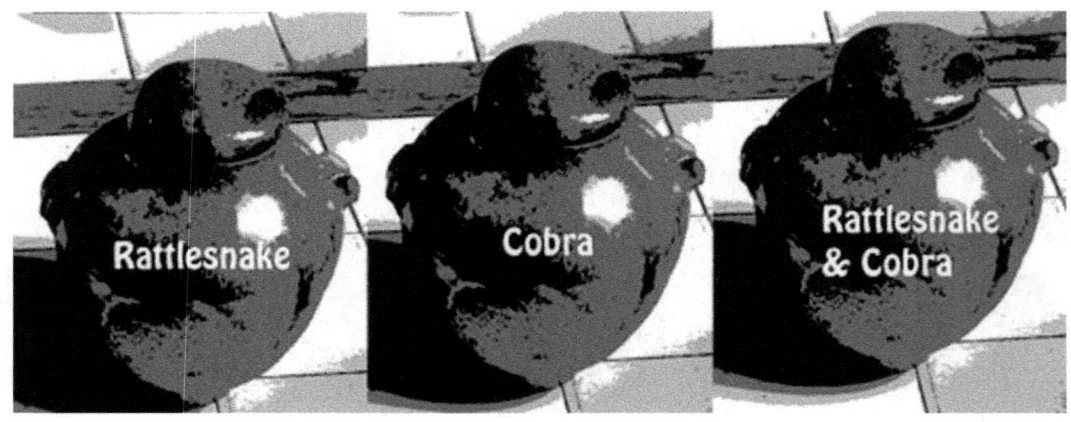

We have three cookie jars. All are covered. One is labeled, 'Rattlesnake and Cobra,' another 'Rattlesnake' and the third 'Cobra.' Poor George, who placed the snakes in the jars is no longer with us. As a parting bit of animosity he informed us that all three jars were labeled incorrectly. George never lied, so we are certain that what he said was the truth.

Now it is your job to label the jars correctly. The jars are too dark to see inside, and no light source is available. The rattlesnakes have had their rattlers removed, so listening won't help you. To top the problem off there is only one vial of antidote for snake bit left. It is good for one bite from either a rattlesnake or a cobra, but only one bite from either of the two.[xx] Since you cannot break the jars and there is no protective equipment available, you must reach into one of the jars and lift a snake out to identify it. From what you learn can you correctly identify what is in what jar?

Two: The Escape Proof Handcuffs and the Unbreakable, Uncuttable, Unburnable Cord

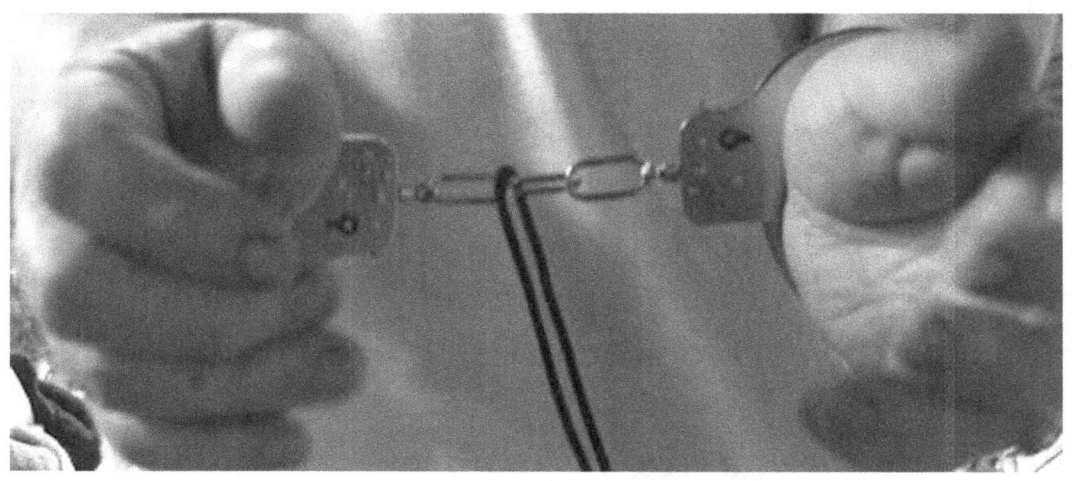

Deputy Simple had to bring Garlic Jim to jail. However he feared Garlic Jim's deadly bad breath. He devised a plan he thought would work. Instead of handcuffing Jim to himself, he handcuffed Jim's hands using escape proof cuffs. Then taking a long piece of super unbreakable, uncuttable, unburnable cord, he looped it once around the chain and holding the two loose ends, marched Jim to jail. So overconfident was Simple that he walked along without ever looking back at his prisoner. Much to Simple's surprise when he got the jail he found Jim gone. Because the cord was still intact and he had never let go the loose ends, Simple concluded that somehow Jim had gotten the escape proof cuffs off. Yet, when they found Jim a few hours later, the handcuffs had not been removed and still held Jim's hands in front of him. How did Jim escape?

 Three: Yes or No

Here is a puzzle for you to try on friends. Tell them this story. "Fred is lying face down on the middle of Miss Lovebody's back yard. He is clutching a toothbrush in his right hand. Poor Fred is quite dead. How did Fred die?"

The object is for your friends to discover the answer by asking questions that can be answered by a simple 'yes' or 'no.' No other type question is allowed. The answer is that Fred was in an airplane, and mistook the emergency exit for the bathroom. Here, watch the approach your friends take to arrive at an answer. You may learn something about ordering your approach to problems.

Watch for the mistakes mentioned in the chapter on symptoms. Make notes of any ideas that come to mind.

Four: Clowney

On the previous page is the picture of a clown. To make the puzzle print the clown on thick photo matt paper filling the page and then cut out completely the portions in GRAY. That is, the two nostril holes and the two separate sections on the mouth. Be careful when cutting out the mouth not to sever the narrow middle section. Then tie a large button or ring (The button or ring must be to large to go through the nostril holes, but not more than 1/2" diameter and 1/4" in width.) to a piece of string or yarn about two feet long.

With one button tied on, lace the string through the holes according to the diagram below. The dotted lines indicate that the string is behind the face of the card.

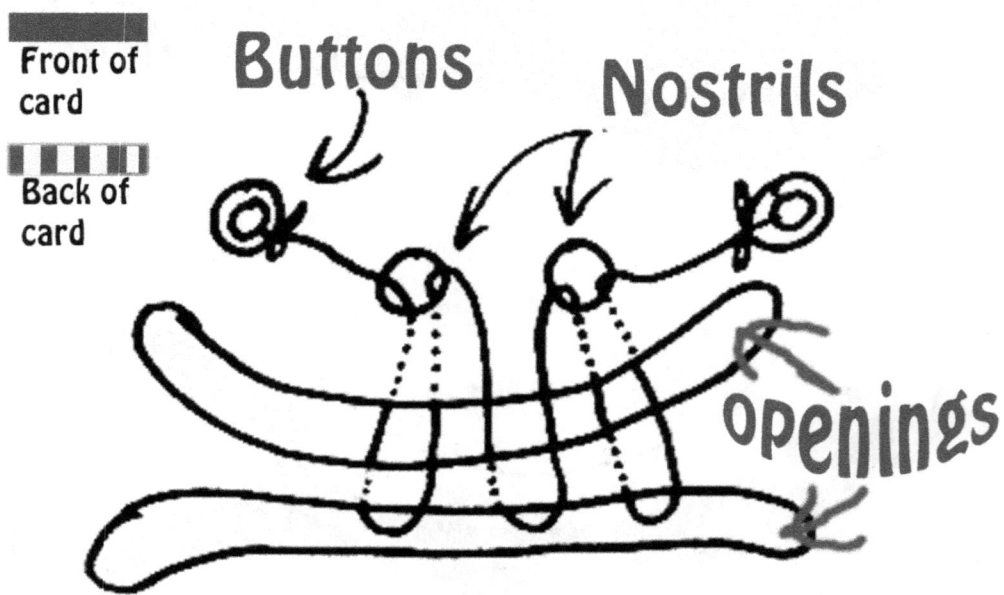

Once laced tie another similar button to the loose end. You should have some play in the string to maneuver with. Can you completely remove the string without tearing or cutting Clowney?

Note: If you get stuck give this to a five year old. They usually solve this very quickly.

Chapter Nine: RELIGIOUS BELIEF AND LOGIC

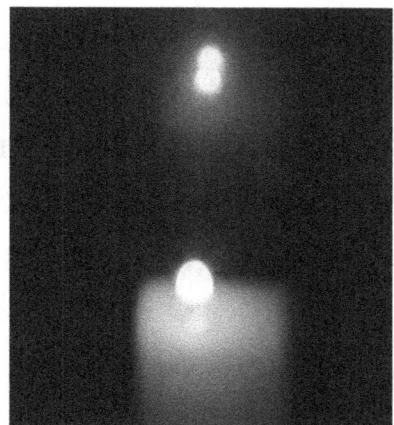

Figure 26. We see a reflection and believe in a candle we can't see.

A mistake a great many of us make which encourages us to think ourselves into lower intelligence is to extend our inability to fathom religious mysteries with the solving of everyday problems.

In any religion there are certain points which are intended to be taken on faith, and should only be taken on faith. These points are not meant to be approached logically, for it they are, they become a challenge to both faith and logic. If we look at the mysteries presented by religion as something requiring knowledge and ability over and above our own, like omnipotence, we will not be so vain as to presume we can solve them all, yet this will not reflect on our intelligence. The danger only arises when we extend this belief to our own world.

What we fail to do in most cases is to place such matters of religious faith in their proper perspective. The problems of faith are on an entirely different plane than the problems of everyday life. We may believe certain concepts of faith that do not agree with logical conclusions. But this does not mean that logic or religion is wrong. In some cases challenging religious concepts logically will take the form of heresy. For those with deep religious convictions, it is a matter for God.

But the fact that we cannot understand a part of our theology in no way means that we cannot understand or solve any problems of this world. The words of Christ in Mathew 22:21 are appropriate here. "Render therefore unto Caesar the things that are Caesars and unto God the things that are God's." Not doing so can be against the principles of some faiths. Mathew 25: 14-30, the parable of the talents is an excellent example of from the bible. Our intelligence is a gift. We must use it and improve upon it to the best of our ability.

Chapter Ten: WOMEN AND INTELLIGENCE

Women are as capable of putting their worlds in order as men are. Men are as capable of putting their worlds in order as women are.

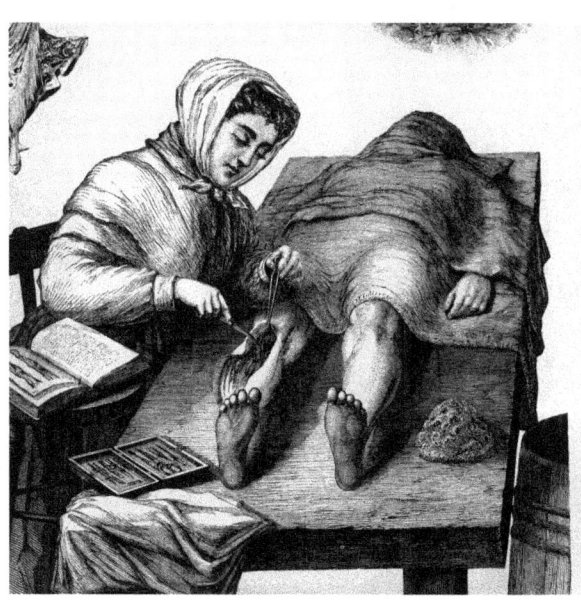

The problem is that in the past women were assigned a certain role in patriarchal societies such as ours. That is they were assigned a certain type of world to order. The problem with assigned roles is that the person assigned a role is often not allowed to access to the world they would like to order.

Some women, of course, have not allowed themselves to be assigned roles. These women stand out in history because of the contributions they've made to the sciences and the arts. Yet, the great waste is what could have been done, had women in the past been given the chance to enrich their minds as diversely as men.

Even today the idea of a role for women is instilled in some young ladies. They are discouraged from competing with males. They are taught their job in life is doing dishes, cleaning house, and having children. They are taught that they will be the housewives and not the breadwinners. If they do go to work they will be assigned roles. They're told to be nurses and not doctors.[xxi]

But roles are a danger because they don't allow an individual to choose the world they can order best. As parents become enlightened, hopefully, the roles will be dropped, and women will be given a more equal chance to order our world.

 For Thought:

Because it is not accurately true, it was not said, 'some girls are brought up to think they are not as smart as men." Why?

How does the mystique of intelligence lead us to judge a woman's role in society?

Chapter Eleven: IQ

IQ stands for "Intelligence Quotient." It is what many consider to be a measure of intelligence. It is a value that shows our achievement, compared to that of others, on an intelligence test. This test is supposed to be an aptitude test, that is a test that will predict how and individual will do in the future. Yet, all intelligence tests measure aptitude by in some way measuring what the test maker has already learned.

Figure 27. Anyone can devise a test that someone else can solve faster then they can, but how do you devise a test to see if someone can think of something you can't even imagine?

The theory of intelligence that allows for an IQ test clearly follows the line, "Some people are more intelligent than others." The problem with the intelligence test is that the test makers place values on certain things, which have been achieved. They decide that some things have more value, show more intelligence than others. This is where the error lies. For instead of a true indication of an ability to put things in order, the intelligence test measures the ability to put in order those things the test makers decided were important enough to put in their test.

Rather than saying, "Some people are more intelligent than others," they should say, "Some people ordered their minds along the lines of our test, more than others." Or, "some people think more like us test makers then others."[xxii] Much of the confusion about intelligence comes from the fact that we judge how an individual has ordered their world by the value we place on the world that has been ordered.

Figure 28. You choose: High IQ, or remember to bring snowshoes?

If we are in need of a brain surgeon we value our brain surgeon's ability more than that of our friend the backwoodsman. Our brain surgeon may have a higher IQ but what if we are lost in the woods?

Chapter Twelve: NOTES ON TEST TAKING

Tests may or may not be accurate indications of intelligence. Intelligence tests are around because we assign values to certain abilities. Now, perhaps it's a good idea to consider the value of the things we intend to order. But one should never limit their idea of their own intelligence by the outcome of any test or series of tests without some self-analysis. Tests tend to be impersonal and can be dangerous because of this.

We may be in a situation some day in which someone else may judge our intelligence or a portion of it by a test.

And so it may be of some benefit to give some notes on test taking.

Some Notes on Test Taking

1) Be prepared! The first and most important thing to do in preparing for a test is to judge the value the test has for you. Underestimating the value of a given test is one of the most common and destructive pitfalls for test takers. Once we decide the value of the test we should do the work necessary to achieve the outcome desired. For any test, become familiar with the type of question to be asked and practice answering them. Practice ordering your approach to them—it can help. One thing test takers often fail to consider are the limitations of the test maker. There is a limit to the number of basic outlines of questions that can be asked on any subject. Individuals who make up tests usually tend to become repetitive after awhile and very often ask the same kinds of questions.
2) Be in condition to take the test. There are people who will do well if they cram the night before a test, but it is a better idea to prepare ahead of time. Learn the information and practice answering questions long before the eve of the test. You hurt only yourself by going into a test in any condition other than your best.

3) Read the directions on the test and be sure you know how to answer the questions. Don't hesitate to ask the test monitor any questions about the instructions if they are not clear to you.
4) Evaluate the test itself. Some questions may be worth more than others. Don't hesitate to ask the test monitor about the value of any questions you are not sure of. Determine how you will answer the questions based on their value and how well you answer them.
5) Be sure to allow time to go over your answers, especially on a multiple-choice test, or check off test. Do this, not only to recheck your answer but to be sure you have indicated the answer you intend.
6) Never allow yourself to become fascinated with, or stuck on, one question. Every once in awhile you will come across a problem that intrigues you. But remember on any test with a time limit you are being graded on your performance, not on what you could do. You may want to tackle an intriguing problem, but to do so would be a waste of precious time.[xxiii] With questions of the same value answer the easiest first. Once these are done, go on to the harder questions. Don't ever waste time on a single question.

 Ideas to Ponder:

If you are not in the habit of being prepared for tests do yourself one favor: keep a notebook. Note what tests you've taken, how you've prepared for them and what the result was. You might keep a diary on how much study you spent on each subject per night. This will give you an indication of how good your system is.

Try making up questions for one particular test. Pick a section on a subject you like and try to think of all the possible questions. (For math just the type of question not every possible number combination.) In this way you'll get an idea of the limits that test makers have to face in creating questions. You'll also get a glimpse of why they always say the best way to learn something is to teach it.

Intelligence tests are administered to young children as well as to older ones. Children may or may not follow the rules. On these tests the fact that they should not spend too much time on one problem is stressed. But wouldn't an intelligent, curious child, if a question were intriguing, break this rule?

Chapter Thirteen: HIGH TEST ANXIETY

We have talked about tests, so perhaps we should mention this also. Although it has no influence on our intelligence directly, it does affect the ideas people may get about our intelligence.

High test anxiety can attack students taking exams,

Figure 29. **High Test Anxiety: Do realize your fear of the deep pool of failure here, could just as easily be a fear of the wide pool of success?**

people not accustomed to speaking in, new drivers taking a road test, or anyone in a test situation. It occurs when people are nervous. They can become so nervous they forget all that they have learned. The only rule is: the more important the test the higher the test anxiety they are likely to have.

The simple solution: Don't be nervous! Easier said than done. The best alternative is to be aware of our anxiety, realize it is a problem and that it may be a reason for failure. And if you fail due to test anxiety don't let the failure discourage you. The fact that many people pass the second road test and get a driver's license is proof that anxiety decreases the second time around.

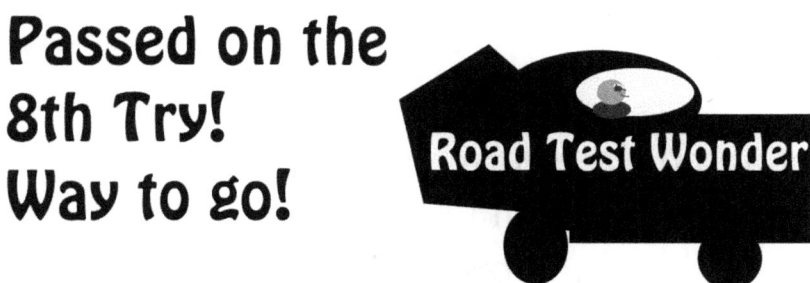

Figure 30. The fact that you passed the road test, no matter how many times it took you, proves you had the ability to pass.

One student taking college entrance exams years ago did not do as well as he liked. He tried his best but his scores were fairly low. With luck he did manage to get into the college of his choice with these scores. It also happened that he had already paid for a second test. There was no way to get the money back, so he took the test again.

Quite differently from his first test, he took his time, looked at the girls, and felt no anxiety.

Figure 31. Don't let fear chase you away from your dreams.

The booklet about the entrance exams stated something to the effect that additional tests would not yield higher scores. They claimed the test was created in such a way that students taking additional tests would score within 25 points of their original scores. Not only were this student's second scores over 100 points higher on both parts, but he had not studies nor prepared for the second test in any way. The only difference was his lack of anxiety.

The stories of high test anxiety are numerous, especially, the ones about those souls who drove perfectly, until seated next to the examiner giving the road test. There is no magic force in curbs making you run over them in the parking test. It is simply high anxiety.

Enough said. We should be aware that high-test anxiety exists and take it for what it is worth. If it happens to you seek another test. Make sure whoever is testing you knows that you can do better. Don't be ashamed of your fear. The fact that you faced the test despite such fear shows exceptional courage. Just be sure, never to imply from a test taken under stress, a limit to your potential ability.

Chapter Fourteen: ANSWERS TO PRACTICE PROBLEMS

One: Snakes

The first thing to do in ordering your approach to this problem is to consider how much you value this job. Then check your life insurance.

If you go ahead you must remember there is only one vial of snakebite antidote. So, you can risk being bitten by only one snake. You know that all the jars are labeled incorrectly. Therefore the only jar you can be sure has only one snake in it is the one that says it has two, 'Rattlesnake and Cobra.'

You reach in and pull out the snake. Suppose it is a 'Cobra.' You know the correct label for this jar is then 'Cobra.' But what of the other two jars? Can you infer from what you've learned how to label them? Well, can the jar actually labeled 'Cobra' contain the 'Rattlesnake and Cobra?'

There are two possible solutions depending on what is in the Rattlesnake & Cobra Jar. The correct snakes are listed beneath each jar on the next page.

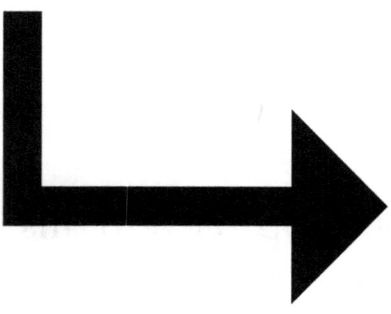

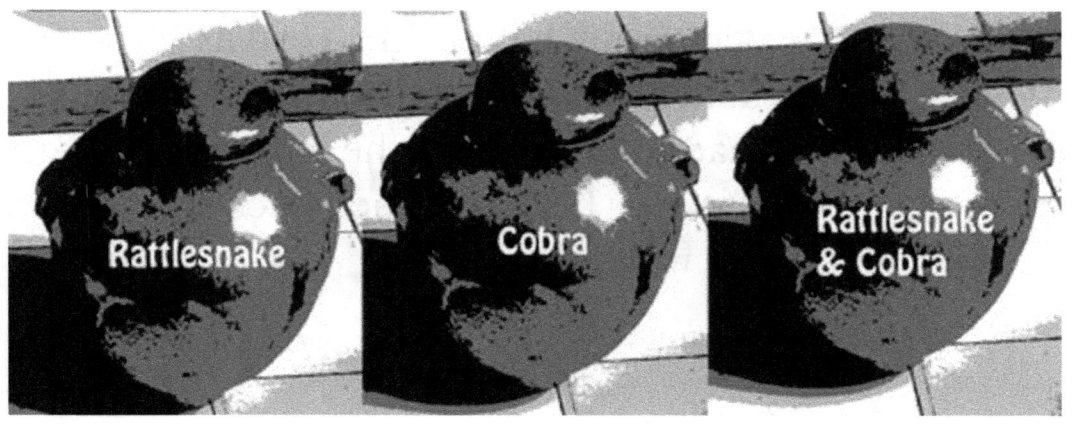

Rattlesnake & Cobra	Rattlesnake	Cobra
Cobra	Rattlesnake & Cobra	Rattlesnake

No. If that were true the jar labeled 'Rattlesnake' would have to be correct because it is the only jar left. So if the 'Cobra' is in the 'Rattlesnake and Cobra' jar then the 'Cobra' jar has to contain the 'Rattlesnake' and the 'Rattlesnake' jar has to contain the 'Rattlesnake and Cobra' if all are labeled incorrectly.

What would the answer be if you found the 'Rattlesnake' in the 'Rattlesnake and Cobra' jar?

Two: The Escape proof Handcuffs and the Unbreakable, Uncuttable, Unburnable Cord.

The handcuffs are not really held by the cord as securely as Deputy Simple imagined. To remove the cord from the cuffs all Garlic had to do was slip the loop underneath one of the cuffs, lift it over his hand, then back through the cuff again and he was free.

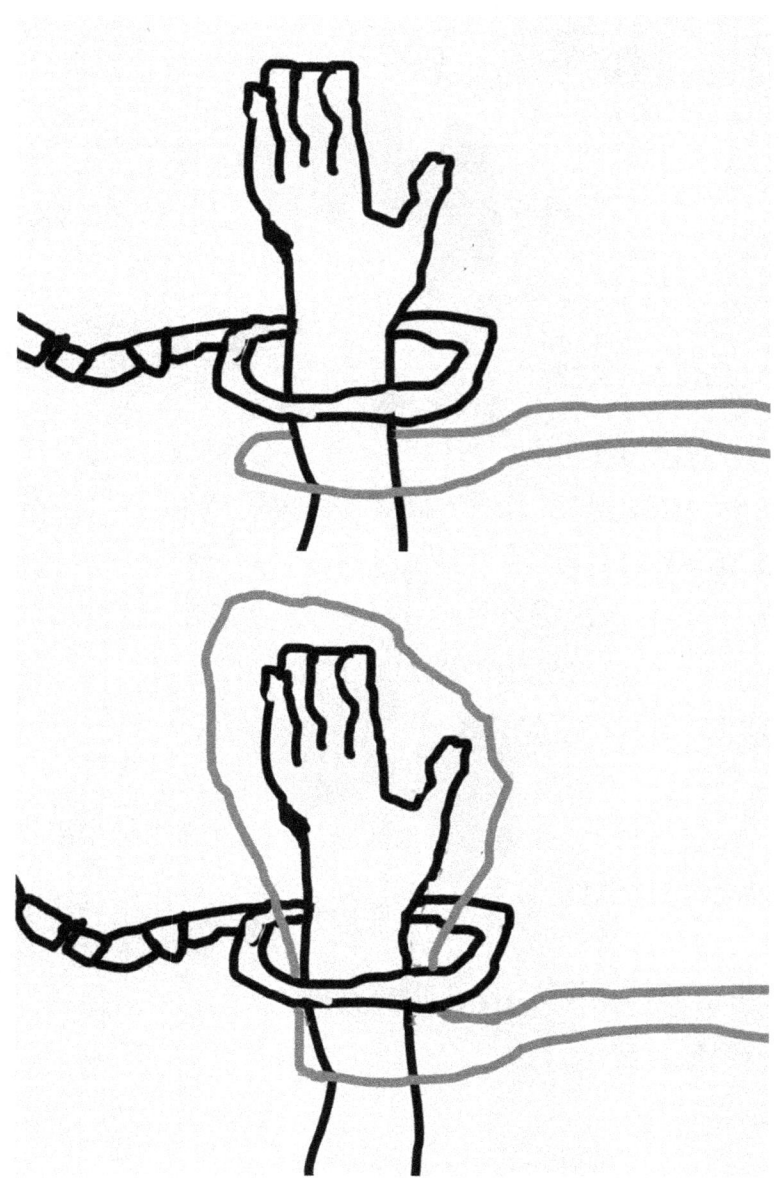

Three: Clowney

To see how easy this is give the puzzle to a five year old. They can solve it very quickly. To remove the string, bend the card so as to bring the thin mouthpiece through the nostril holes (one at a time). You can then slip the buttons through these nostril loops and free the string without destroying clowney.

CONCLUSION

We are thinking ourselves into lower intelligence if we ignore the possibilities of our own potential for using our intelligence. If we believe that there are ideas we cannot understand or problems we cannot solve we are cheating ourselves. No matter how complex a problem or idea may be, if we are interested enough, have the time to experiment or explore, adding any additional information we may need on the way, there is no reason why we should fail. And with each success we should be confident that each additional attempt will be easier.

---

[i] An idea can be more time consuming to understand, but if you can understand the language….

[ii] This teacher kept emphasizing that math was easy, because he realized most students had problems because they imagined math to be harder than it really is. Later the student while teaching advanced calculus, himself, as a substitute teacher would use the same principle. Most of the student's students earned A's.

[iii] Oddly English professors are the worst when it comes to putting others down. They don't call it the Department of Anguish for nothing. Computer science geeks on the other hand can be very nice, take time to explain things, and have no need to feel superior. Keep in mind that there are few English teaching jobs, and competition is cutthroat. Meanwhile, everyone who is good at computer science can find a good job. (I have been a graduate student in both English and Computer science.)

[iv] For me, mechanical things daunted me the most. Before I read ZEN AND THE ART OF MOTORCYLE MAINTENANCE (actually a novel) I assumed fixing mechanical things was beyond me. Nowhere in the books on repair did they explain what to do when a nut is frozen or strips. But frozen bolts, stripped nuts, and disintegrating screw heads seemed to be the norm for me. I let such incidents convince me that I was incapable of mechanical work. This was partly due to having had such bad experiences when I was younger and physically incapable of overcoming the problem. I've since learned I can do almost anything, and even have published videos on mechanical topics.

[v] Or perhaps don't consider any question stupid.

[vi] Actually, we have an built in predisposition for communication, i.e. we would invent language if our parents weren't waiting for us with it already defined. The invention is the nuances invoked by culture, etc, and therein the problem lies.

[vii] I was substitute teaching and some students in a math class were agonizing over a computer progam that just would not work after weeks of programming. I found the bug instantly, they forgot to put a slash before an apostrophe. It was a one character error in thousands of lines of code. Don't let life's little stop-you-in-your-tracks errors get you down! The more mistakes you make the smarter you'll be!

[viii] Not to be confused with emotional "Crazymakers." People who cause uproars just for the emotional kick. Or those who use extreme passive-aggressive behavior.

[ix] The worst teacher I ever had was when I was a graduate student in computer science. This teacher never prepared for class, just thought he could wing it, and never evaluated the assignments he gave from the text (i.e. for the amount of time it would take to solve or complete them.)

[x] Try looking up the second law of thermodynamics.

[xi] High school teachers certainly feel that way. But even that feeling can be suspect.

[xii] When we say people we are talking groups and the problem with groups is shown by the math paradox: Our social selves are more than suspect when it comes to math. Try this if you have about 20 people in a classroom. Give them this problem:
A farmer buys a horse for $60. He sells it for $70, but then finds he could have made a better deal. He borrows $10 from his wife and buys it back for $80. He then sells it for $90. How much money does he make. Most groups will divide on the answer. Get the people who agree on an amount into their own groups and have each group argue for their answer. There is, by the way, only one correct answer.

[xiii] We may not always be physically up to par which affects our mental ability. Have you ever watched an answer game show like JEOPARDY while tired, and could not come up with an answer you knew you knew.

[xiv] All of the Holmes stories and novels taken as a whole. If you are a fan and looking for a complete collection I strongly recommend The Annotated Sherlock Holmes by William S. Baring-Gould.

[xv] For a parallel true story read The Tracker by Tom Brown, Jr.

[xvi] Many, many years ago I took a sort of combination dexterity/recognition test. The answer card was a grid where multiple choice answers were blacked out with a pencil. The way the test was arranged I concluded that rather than answer across the rows as the questions were numbered, I answered in columns which was much more efficient. They failed me. The moral, never try to out-think the person who devised the grading system for a test.

[xvii] This is an example of a hoax puzzle. Draw six balls.
0 0 0
0 0 0
The object is to connect with a pencil line, each ball to every other ball without crossing lines. It is impossible in two dimensions. It drove me crazy when I was in grammar school.

[xviii] The hoax in this case would be someone hid them on us.

[xix] I am grateful to the originators of these and all the authors of puzzles I've read over the years, and especially, my old friend Larry Tricerri who drove me crazy with his puzzles years ago, and helped seed the idea that became this book.

[xx] Rattlesnake venom and Cobra Venom are completely different but this is just a puzzle.

[xxi] My daughter graduated in the top ten of her high school in a class of 500. She had had a part-time job in the principal's office. This idiot male music teacher got up at graduation to give her an award and said, 'she'll make someone a fine secretary.'

[xxii] I was teaching myself C++ programming and for fun tried some of the questions in a entrance exam sample for law school. The computer found an error in a question about how long it would take to do graduate recitals at a music school. The question, which basically evaluated whether the test taker thought like other lawyers,

failed to consider that recitals could be carried out at the same time in different rooms.

[xxiii] When I was a research chemist at Revlon there were always interesting avenues to explore. But in my years there we only invented one new product. The rest of the time we were 'new and improving' old products on a deadline schedule. There was little time for solving chemical puzzles that would not make a profit.

www.ingramcontent.com/pod-product-compliance
Lightning Source LLC
Chambersburg PA
CBHW081356040426
42451CB00017B/3468